WHAT'S FASTER THAN A SPEEDING CHEETAH?

Robert E. Wells

Albert Whitman & Company • Morton Grove, Illinois

For my wife, Karen: your love and encouragement are always appreciated.

Also by Robert E. Wells
Is a Blue Whale the Biggest Thing There Is?
What's Smaller Than a Pygmy Shrew?
How Do You Lift a Lion?

Library of Congress Cataloging-in-Publication Data

Wells, Robert E.
What's faster than a speeding cheetah? / written and
illustrated by Robert E. Wells.
p.   cm.
Summary: Compares the speeds of various animals, from
humans to cheetahs to peregrine falcons, with even
faster things like rockets, meteoroids, and light.
ISBN 0-8075-2280-5 (hardcover)
ISBN 0-8075-2281-3 (paperback)
1. Speed—Juvenile literature. [1. Speed.] I. Title.
QC137.52.W45   1997   96-54491
531'.112—dc21   CIP
                                                  AC

Hand-lettering by Robert E. Wells.
The illustration media are pen and acrylic.
Design by Susan B. Cohn.

You may very well be fast on your feet. But if you want to WIN races, never race a CHEETAH- or even an OSTRICH, for that matter.

If you ran very hard, you might reach a speed of 15 miles per hour.

That's not nearly fast enough to keep up with an ostrich. With a top speed of about 45 miles per hour, an ostrich is the world's fastest 2-legged runner.

But the cheetah will certainly be way out in front.

A cheetah can reach a speed of about 70 miles per hour – MORE THAN A MILE A MINUTE!

No animal on EARTH can run faster than that!

But a cheetah can't run nearly as fast as a PEREGRINE FALCON can SWOOP!

A peregrine falcon is truly a SUPER SWOOPER.

It can dive faster than any creature can run.

FINISH

But not as fast as
an AIRPLANE can fly!

Some propeller planes can fly more than **300** miles per hour.

With a propeller pulling you through the air, you can travel faster than the fastest falcon.

But with a JET ENGINE, you can fly faster than the fastest propeller plane – and even faster than the SPEED OF SOUND!

If you shouted a message to someone who was traveling faster than sound, your voice would not go fast enough to ever catch up to him, so he would never hear it!

Flying through the air in a jet
is a mighty fast way to travel.

But if you want to travel to the MOON, you're going to need something that's much, MUCH faster.

You're going to need a ROCKET SHIP!

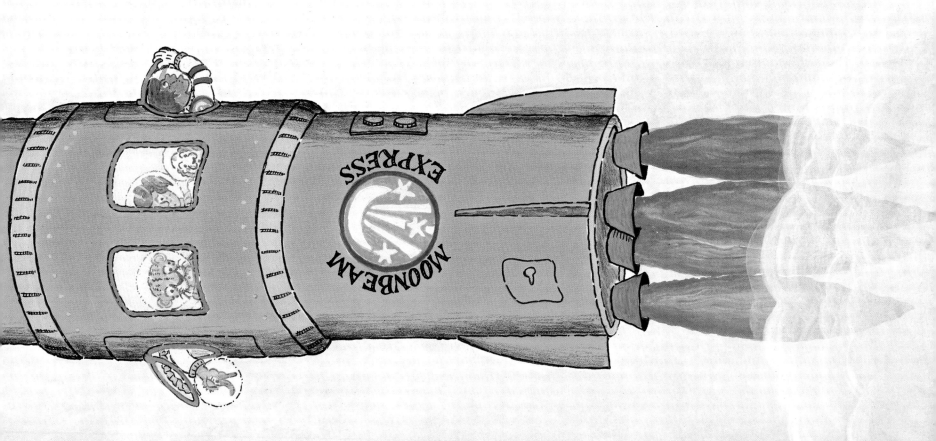

To escape Earth's gravity and travel into space, a rocket ship must travel faster than the fastest jet.

To travel all the way to the moon, a rocket ship must reach a speed of about 25,000 MILES PER HOUR—MORE THAN 30 TIMES AS FAST AS SOUND!

You can turn off your rockets and COAST after you're in space, because there's no air friction.

IT'S A METEOROID!

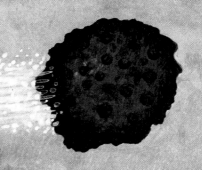

A meteoroid is a space rock. Some meteoroids streak through space at 150,000 miles per hour— SIX TIMES FASTER THAN YOUR ROCKET SHIP IS TRAVELING!

As you circle around the moon and head back to Earth, you might be thinking that the meteoroid you saw was the absolute fastest thing you could ever see.

But hold on a minute. There's something much faster than even the fastest meteoroid — and it's something you see all the time.

Just push the switch on a FLASHLIGHT.

At that speed, you could circle the Earth MORE THAN 7 TIMES IN ONE SECOND!

Instantly, a LIGHT BEAM will flash out at the amazing speed of 186,000 miles per SECOND!

That's THOUSANDS of times FASTER THAN A METEOROID!

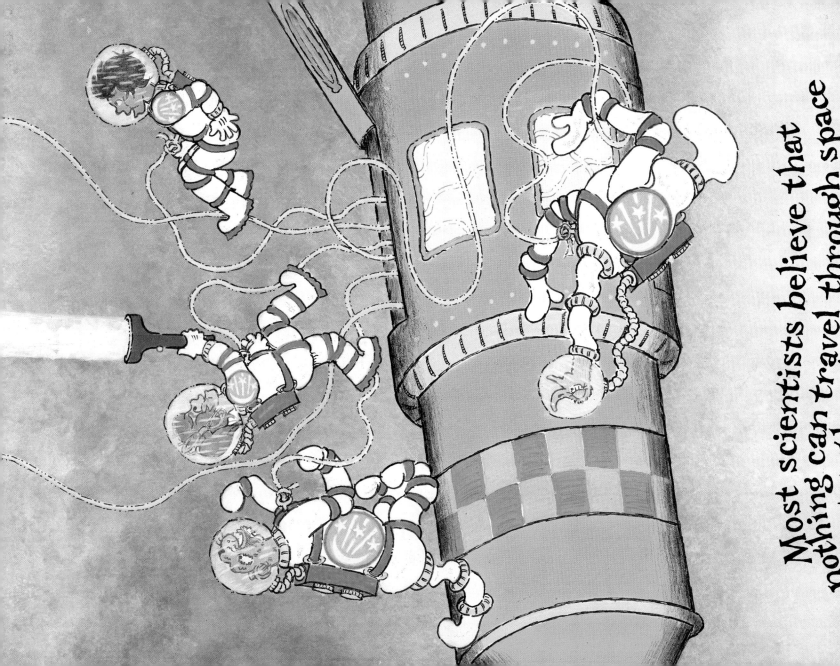

Most scientists believe that nothing can travel through space faster than light.

Who ever would have thought that the FASTEST TRAVELING THING IN THE WHOLE UNIVERSE could come out of something small enough to hold in your hand?

Some Additional Thoughts on Very Fast Things

Sometimes speeds are hard to measure. Observers often have trouble measuring the speeds of wild animals, so books may have numbers that differ. The figures given in this book seem to be the best estimates. It would be much simpler if cheetahs, ostriches, and falcons came with speedometers!

The speed of sound through air is easier to measure than the speeds of wild animals. But the speed of sound is not constant. It's about 760 miles per hour at sea level but slows to about 660 miles per hour at high altitudes where the air is thin and cold.

Meteoroids zoom through space at different speeds, too. The meteoroid in this book is one of the faster ones.

The amazing speed of light, traveling through space at 186,000 miles per second, is one of the few speeds you can count on to be constant.

All the speeds in this book are true to life, but some liberties were taken in the illustrations to better show speed comparisons. In the real world, supersonic jets fly much higher than little propeller planes. And large meteoroids don't often narrowly miss rocket ships!

Although light beams flashing through space are usually shown as bright rays, as is the one in this book, a real light beam becomes bright and visible only when hitting such things as dust or water particles. Fortunately, our space travelers happened to be zooming through a big cloud of space dust just as they switched on their flashlight!

AT THIS SPEED	HOW LONG WOULD IT TAKE TO TRAVEL
YOUNG RUNNER (15 MILES PER HOUR)	
OSTRICH (45 MPH)	
CHEETAH (70 MPH)	
PEREGRINE FALCON (200 MPH)	
PROPELLER PLANE (300 MPH)	
SUPERSONIC JET (1400 MPH)	
ROCKET SHIP (25,000 MPH)	
METEOROID (150,000 MPH)	
LIGHT (186,000 MILES PER SECOND)	

FROM THE EARTH TO THE MOON?
(ABOUT 239,000 MILES)

IT WOULD TAKE ABOUT
1¾ YEARS
7⅓ MONTHS
4⅔ MONTHS
7 WEEKS
4⅔ WEEKS
1 WEEK
9½ HOURS
1½ HOURS
1⅓ SECONDS

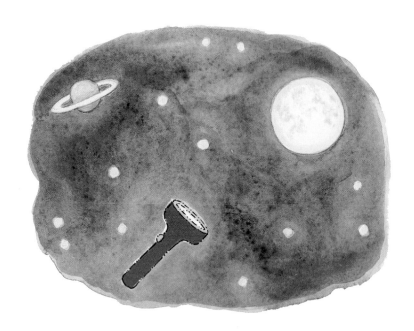